MAKING GOD'S
GOOD NEWS
KNOWN

T.M. MOORE

"The Lord hath made known his salvation: his righteousness hath he openly showed in the sight of the heathen." Psalm 98:2

GREAT COMMISSION PUBLICATIONS

7401 OLD YORK ROAD, PHILADELPHIA, PENNSYLVANIA 19126

ISBN 0-934688-18-4

Scripture quotations are from the HOLY BIBLE,
NEW INTERNATIONAL VERSION. Copyright © 1973,
1978, 1984 by International Bible Society.
Used by permission.

Copyright © 1985 by Frank C. Horton
Second printing 1988

Printed in USA

Published by Great Commission Publications
7401 Old York Road, Philadelphia, Pennsylvania 19126

TABLE OF CONTENTS

Author's Note

This study has been designed as an introduction to evangelism in the local church. My hope is that students will find enough information and practical instruction here to excite them to become better equipped for their God-given mandate as witnesses for Jesus Christ in their everyday lives. This book should not be seen as a substitute for more-concentrated preparation for evangelism. This is available through other vehicles and agencies. I am grateful to Dr. D. James Kennedy, pastor of the Coral Ridge Presbyterian Church in Ft. Lauderdale, Florida and president of Evangelism Explosion III, International, for his permission to reproduce the outline of the gospel which appears in his book, *Evangelism Explosion* (Wheaton: Tyndale House, 1983, third edition), throughout this study.

T. M. Moore
Ft. Lauderdale, Florida

1

What Is God's Good News?

This book introduces the subject of evangelism and describes its place in the life of the individual believer and its role in the work of the local church. In recent years churches in the evangelical tradition have had something of an on-again off-again relationship with personal evangelism. Since reaching a peak in the mid-1970s enthusiasm for personal witnessing seems to have entered a period of decline. Other church-based interests and ministries have appeared, most of them sorely needed, which have served to overshadow the importance of getting the good news of Jesus Christ out to the lost.

This book is but a feeble effort toward redressing this situation. There are indications that interest in personal witnessing is beginning to rise again among evangelical churches all over the world. My hope is to stimulate that interest by providing a general introduction to the importance of understanding God's good news and of committing and preparing ourselves to make it known.

We begin then by asking the obvious question, "What is God's good news?"

God's Good News Is God's

The apostle Peter put it this way in explaining to his readers the origin of his message:

> For we have not followed cunningly devised fables, when we made known unto you the power and coming of our Lord Jesus Christ, but were eyewitnesses of his majesty. For he received from God the Father honour and glory, when there came such a voice to him from the excellent glory, This is my beloved Son, in whom I am well pleased. And this voice which came from heaven we heard, when we were with him in the holy mount. We have also a more sure word of prophecy; whereunto ye do well that ye take heed (2 Pet. 1:16–19).

Peter wanted his readers to be sure that they understood the divine origin of the message that they believed. God's good news is, above all else, God's. This means first that it comes from him. The gospel is not the product of human imagination, nor even of the best and brightest theological or philosophical minds. Its origin is in the councils of heaven where, before the creation, the Father, Son and Holy Spirit covenanted together for the salvation of a people for God (Eph. 1:4). Thus the message carries divine authorization each time it is spoken. No wonder we are promised that it will not return to God without accomplishing his purpose (Is. 55:11).

The fact that God's good news is God's also indicates that it is centered in him. The gospel is about God. It tells us about who he is, what he requires of us, and what he has accomplished to bring us into a right relationship with him. The gospel is not, in the first place, about meeting human needs or delivering us from whatever encumbers us. The gospel is about God, which is why the apostle John could say of Jesus' mission that "the only begotten Son, which is in the bosom of the Father, he hath declared him"—that is, God (John 1:18). Thus this gospel takes away the need to be perfect since it centers not in who we are but in who God is and what he has done for us.

Further, God's good news is God's because it relates back to him. The gospel is not merely an instrument for bringing peace or prosperity. The gospel is the means by which men and women are restored to right relationship with God and begin to enjoy the fruits and benefits of fellowship with him (Rom. 5:1; 1 Cor. 3:21–23). Our gospel has not been fully declared until it focuses attention on the beauties and mysteries of God.

We must, then, understand from the beginning that the message with which we are concerned is above all else God's, formulated on his terms, accomplished in his time and according to his design, and purposed to draw men and women to himself and his glory.

God's Good News Is Good

We need also to understand that the gospel is good news. Its intended effects are good all the way around, in spite of the efforts of detractors to make it out as a cumbersome and archaic notion. God's good news is good first because it informs us of what pleases and satisfies God. Once we know the good news we know that God's wrath is satisfied once for all. There is no need for us to fear that an angry deity will reach down into time and destroy us. The good news tells us that God has found good in what he has accomplished for salvation (Rom. 8.1).

God's good news is good also because it tells humans what they need to hear in order to be delivered from their desperate condition of sin, darkness, uncertainty and fear. It tells those who are strangers and aliens and who have no hope in this life that there is meaning, purpose, joy, peace—in short, good news—in the saving message of Christ (Eph. 2:12–14).

Moreover God's good news is good in that it works to bring many into a new and exciting relationship with God. The gospel is effective for the salvation of those who believe. It catapults them into an entirely new manner of living. They are "born again" (Rom. 1:16, 17).

Thus not only is the gospel of divine origin and design, it is filled with truly good news for all concerned. Certainly here is a message which we can proclaim with confidence and enthusiasm to a beleaguered world.

God's Good News Is News

This may sound like a tautology, but let us have a somewhat closer look. God's good news is news. It breaks in upon us unexpectedly. None of us ever truly goes about seeking God. As Paul reminded us from the Psalms, "There is none that understandeth, there is none that seeketh after God" (Rom. 3:11). Thus any who find God—or should we say, are found of God—do so serendipitously when in his sovereign grace he sends a messenger to speak it to their hardened hearts.

Furthermore the gospel is news in that it changes every aspect of our lives. Nothing can be the same when the gospel has been received. It cannot be more succinctly put then Paul has done: "If any man be in Christ, he is a new creature: old things are passed away; behold, all things are become new" (2 Cor. 5:17). The gospel begins to leaven every aspect of human life and interest. It reforms and remakes ideas, aspirations, roles and relationships with a power from on high that works within.

Finally the gospel is news in that it is announced. As the prophet Amos put it, "The Lord God hath spoken, who can but prophesy?" (Amos 3:8). We who are recipients of the good news of Jesus Christ are blessed with the riches of God. How can we be silent in the face of what God has done? How can we fail to make God's good news known?

What Is God's Good News?

At this point let's look at a summary of the gospel. There are many ways of arranging its distinctive features. One which thousands of believers have found helpful in learning to announce God's good news takes the following form:

GRACE
- Eternal life is a free gift.
- It is not earned or deserved.

MAN
- Man is a sinner.
- He cannot save himself.

GOD
- God is merciful.
- God is just and must punish sin.

JESUS CHRIST
- He is the infinite, eternal God/Man.
- He came to die on a cross and purchase a place for us in heaven.

FAITH
- Faith is the key to heaven.
- It is not mere intellectual belief or temporal faith, but trusting in Jesus Christ alone for salvation.

Accepting this simple message has introduced unnumbered men and women from all places and times, all races and tongues, and all walks of life to a new dimension of living, a new understanding of the world, and a new zeal for life and for the glory of God. The burden of making God's good news known has been passed from generation to generation. Now it has fallen like an unavoidable gauntlet at the feet of today's Christians. How will we respond to this glorious good news and our mandate to make it known among the men and women of our generation?

Review Questions

1. Where does the origin of the gospel lie?
2. Who is the primary focus of the gospel?
3. What is the gospel intended to accomplish?
4. What does the gospel accomplish with respect to the wrath of god?
5. How does the gospel come to individual men and women?
6. Who is commissioned to proclaim the gospel to a lost world?
7. What are the five main points of the gospel message?

Discussion Questions

1. Why is it important to understand that the gospel is of divine origin and design? How should this affect our witnessing?

2. What does the gospel accomplish for you? Can you give some examples from your personal life as to how you have experienced these benefits?

3. Take a moment to read out loud the main points and sub-points of the gospel message, either to yourself or in a small group. When you have finished that, close the book and do it again, trying from memory to say as much of the message as possible. (It will be good for you to memorize this basic message as soon as possible.)

4. Knowing that the gospel is truly good news, why do

so few Christians ever do much personal witnessing? Is there anything inherent in the gospel itself to help overcome these problems?

2

What Makes God's Good News Good?

We have seen that God's good news is of divine origin and design and that it comes to us at his initiative to bind us back to himself. The gospel message is filled with meaning and importance for modern men and women. It is the power of God to deliver from misery, despair and sin. We want to take a closer look at this dimension of the gospel in this chapter. The gospel is good news principally because of its beneficial effect on human lives.

The Plight of Modern Man

We live in an age unlike any other before it. Ours is an age that has actively sought to sever itself from the heritage of religious tradition that was for centuries its foundation and its overriding strength. Never before has there been an age that sought to chart its course on a purely secular, this-worldly basis. The effects of this commitment have been devastating.

Uncountable are the men and women whose lives are teetering on the brink of annihilation because they have no sure foundation for the decisions and choices they must make each day. They drift on the tides of whim and consensus, never knowing from one year to the next which morals, which beliefs or which practices will find acceptance among the members of their group. Many are overcome with anxiety and a plethora of physical ills that replace each other seemingly without end.

The people of our age have watched their familiar traditions dissolve in a sea of relativism. They have witnessed attack after attack against their institutions and leaders. They have felt the erosion of their moral foundations, all the while looking desperately for somewhere certain to leap. Their searching eyes and outstretched arms find only other people who struggle to get through yet another day.

Is it any wonder that modern artists paint figures of disintegrating human beings, boxed in and screaming? Or that modern song writers pen the sounds of silence or the fleeting sensuality of sex and power? Or that our writers portray impermanence, relativity and despair as the common themes of mankind? Our age in flight from God is in deep trouble. It is in desperate need of some good news to keep it from what Malcolm Muggeridge has described as the inevitable inclination to commit suicide.

It is in the midst of this terrible plight that the gospel of Jesus Christ presents such opportunities for meaning and hope.

WHAT MAKES GOD'S GOOD NEWS GOOD?

The Power of the Gospel

The apostle Paul described God's good news as "the power of God unto salvation" (Rom. 1:16). What makes the gospel such tremendous good news for modern men is that it delivers them from their plight. A number of well-known reprobates, criminals and assorted ne'er-do-wells, coming to faith in Jesus Christ, have had their lives forever rescued and reformed by the transforming power of the gospel. How is it that this simple message of grace and forgiveness can have such an incredible effect?

The gospel is powerful to save because it deals effectively with the problem of sin. All the ills of modern men and women are directly tied to the sin which pervades their lives like a terminal disease. In Genesis 3 the introduction of sin and disobedience is accompanied by psychological trauma, relational distress, physical pain and turmoil, and self-seeking of a high order. Only when that sin was forgiven (symbolized by God's providing a covering of skins, a covering provided at the cost of blood) could Adam and Eve settle down to work out a normal life together in harmony and love. Only forgiveness through the blood of Jesus Christ can empower modern men and women to escape secularism and begin the life that they were created to enjoy.

Once received, the gospel becomes a new foundation, a new reference point and a new power for a life of meaning and purpose. The message of the gospel is good news because it delivers men and women from their self-induced plight. It opens up the treasures of heaven and eternity in the here and now. This is perhaps best fathomed in the uncanny ability of the gospel to bring peace.

The Peace That Passes Understanding

If there is one consistent testimony that comes from those who have received Jesus Christ it is of the gospel's ability to flood their lives with peace. Paul declared that we have peace with God through the gospel (Rom. 5:1). The gospel brings peace instead of hostility (Eph. 2:14). The peace of the gospel guards our hearts and minds in the midst of the most pressing challenges (Phil. 4:7).

Surely this good news will be appealing to the men and women of our generation. No more the need to fret and worry over everyday affairs: Jesus will supply every need and bring us his peace. Gone the jealousy and suspicion which characterize the normal relationships of people: Jesus shows us how to find fulfillment in him and to reach out to others in love. No more the dread of death and destruction: Jesus is preparing a place of eternal rest and peace for all who trust in him.

Making God's good news known is one of the most urgent tasks of the Christian community. Like those lepers of old who, stumbling upon food and water to feed their starving flesh, rebuked themselves for failing to consider the needs of their countrymen in the city (2 Kings 7:3–11), so we need to rouse ourselves from our self-satisfied complacency and resolve to begin making God's good news known to the men and women around us. A dying generation in an age of dying dreams will listen gladly to the good news of life and peace which we bring.

Review Questions

1. What lies at the heart of all of modern man's problems and fears?

2. What is it that makes our age different from any which has preceded it?

3. Where does the power of the gospel begin in dealing with the problems facing modern man?

4. What three types of peace are provided through the gospel?

5. How does the gospel overcome the fear of death?

6. What is our responsibility to our fellow men and women when it comes to speaking the gospel?

Discussion Questions

1. What forms does the plight of modern man take in the realm of the individual? Of relationships between individuals? Of international affairs?

2. What are some of the schemes which men and women devise to extricate themselves from their problems? What does Prov. 14:12 say about such schemes?

3. What do you imagine will be required of us in order to get modern men and women to begin listening to the message of God's good news? Do we simply need to start talking it up or is there more required for us if we are to be believed?

4. Turn back to chapter 1 and the message of the gospel

outlined there. Have you memorized this yet? If so, take some time now to say it out loud either to yourself or in a small group. If not, repeat the exercise given at the end of chapter 1 for this.

3

Who Needs God's Good News?

By now we should be getting a somewhat clearer idea as to just how important God's good news is for contemporary men and women. Anything which has such divine origins and purposes and such power to deliver from sin and its ills is of the utmost significance.

Yet, as we look at people, many of them seem quite unconcerned about either the gospel or the relativistic context in which they are seeking to carve out an existence. In fact many of these men and women appear to be quite happy and content. Could it be that their plight is not as desperate as we have portrayed it? Could it be that they do not really need God's good news?

In order to answer these questions we need to take one step backward by reminding ourselves of something we discussed in our last chapter.

God's Good News Delivers from Sin

We need to keep in mind that the primary intent of the gospel is twofold. First, it tells us that God has provided an atonement for mankind's violation of his law. The shed blood of Jesus Christ satisfied the demands of God. He accepts Jesus' work in our place (cf. 2 Cor. 5:21). From God's point of view the work of Christ has effectively dealt with the sin of those who believe. Surely this is good news.

Second, the purpose of the gospel is to communicate the benefits of God's mercy to those who believe. It informs them that their just condemnation has been removed and, in its place, eternal life has been given (Rom. 6:23).

Thus the gospel effectively addresses and resolves the problem of human sin. Its full saving effect appears in the life of the individual as he works out God's salvation in a life of good works and peace (Phil. 2:12, 13; Eph. 2:10, 14).

The beauty of the gospel, then, is in its ability to overcome the effects of sin in our lives. We need to understand that these effects are pervasive.

Sin Affects the Whole of Life

Regardless of whether or not the terrible effects of sin are outwardly visible in the life of a man or woman, the Scriptures are clear that its impact is radical. A brief look at Paul's summary of those effects will show this.

In Rom. 3:12–18 Paul catalogues the effects of sin in human life. He observes that sin diverts men and women from the path for which they were created by God (vs. 12). That diversion from divine purpose may seem, in any particular instance, only a little departure. However, carried out consistently over time, it causes one to miss the mark entirely and to stray steadily farther from God's course.

Paul also observes that the effects of this straying make everything such people do of no benefit. Being off the prescribed course, no step in their walk can be expected to have God's approval. He may do good through them for the sake of others, but this is in spite of their straying and does not accrue any eternal benefit to themselves.

He next observes that sin affects the speech of those who have departed from God's way (vs. 13). Their conversation, because it does not point to a glorious God, does not reflect his dignity and compassion but seeks only the aggrandizement of the individual, is filthy, deceitful, harmful and often disparaging of others (vs. 14). Since they are bound to a course which separates them increasingly from God's guidance it is to be expected that their speech will reflect their drift.

Furthermore their actions are self-seeking and tend to the ruin of others (vss. 15, 16). Though their assaults against the integrity of others may be only slight—even unintentional—their effects are often devastating. How many hurts and lasting scars are inflicted by those who, seeking only their own benefit, trample the feelings, desires or needs of others under foot!

It is no wonder that such people are unable to provide others or themselves with the real peace that they so desperately need (vs. 17). Even though they may not outwardly show need for the gospel of peace it is certain that, deep within, their spirits are crying out for rest in the midst of growing uncertainty and doubt.

Their basic problem is that there is no fear of God before their eyes (vs. 18). Having strayed from the only path that can lead them to God, unable and unwilling to return, they seldom give his concerns or demands a second thought. Reasonably content with the life they have managed to make for themselves they press ahead, fearing only the unknown future and the certainty of the grave.

What they do not understand is that God's good news rectifies all this and points to a course which has its culmination in fellowship with God. Instead, trapped in consequences of their own choosing, they sense the lurking shadow of uncertainty around every corner. Who are these people thus committed to a course of destruction and despair?

Every One Is a Sinner

Paul gives us the answer to this question in the same passage. His words, not the appearances which meet our eyes, must guide our understanding of the world.

Paul puts it succinctly: "All have sinned, and come short of the glory of God" (vs. 23); "they are all under sin" (vs. 9); "There is none righteous, no, not one" (vs. 10); "There is none that seeketh after God" (vs. 11).

We must agree that these remarks are all-inclusive. There is not a man or woman who has ever lived who has not been found wanting in God's eyes. No matter how prosperous, content, moral or decent an individual may appear, deep within the heart there lurks sin which comes to expression from time to time. Though their diversions from the path of God's law may seem slight, over the long haul they are on a course of everlasting destruction.

Sin, as we have seen, spreads out to infect the whole of a person's life, cutting him off from fellowship with God, whose eyes are too pure to look on evil (Is. 59:2; Hab. 1:13). Only the gospel of Jesus Christ can rescue such a person from this plight, "for there is none other name under heaven given among men whereby we must be saved" (Acts 4:12).

Everyone Needs God's Good News

It is clear that every living person needs to hear the good news of God's forgiveness and love in Jesus Christ. This applies in the remotest villages and jungles, where the church sends missionaries to declare the gospel to primitive tribes, as well as in the metropolis, where faithful preachers call the lost to repentance and faith.

But it also applies to the people we see each day—the people who pump our gas, deliver our mail, bag our groceries, work in our offices, attend our social clubs and live in our neighborhoods. And it has never been God's intent that such people should have to be reached by missionaries or preachers. Instead God has designed a much more attractive, much more effective, method of bringing his good news to them. He sends you and me to exemplify and declare his love for lost sinners. If God's good news is to be made known to today's generation it will require our availability to him as witnesses to Jesus Christ.

Review Questions

1. What is the twofold purpose of the gospel?
2. Give some examples of how sin affects the whole of one's life.
3. Who does Paul say is to be found under the condemnation of sin? Are any excluded?
4. Should we assume that people who appear to be prosperous and content do not need to hear the gospel? Why or why not?
5. Who can you think of right now that need to hear God's good news?
6. Who is the most likely candidate to share that good news with those people?

Discussion Questions

1. What different kinds of things do people turn to in order to keep from having to face up to the hopelessness and uncertainty that haunt them?

2. What evidence do you see in the modern world of the truth of Paul's catalogue of the effects of sin?

3. What is the difference between the law of sin and individual sins? What is their relationship?

4. Take some time to practice saying the outline of the gospel which was presented at the end of the first chapter. By now you should have all five points and the subpoints memorized.

4

Who Has God's Good News?

It is precisely because of the desperate condition in which human beings find themselves that God sent his only Son and gave his gospel in order that they might be saved. His love for sinners goes far beyond our ability to comprehend, for he loved us even while we were his enemies (Col. 1:21, 22). He has brought his good news to bear upon our lives in a powerful and life-changing way. We are the ones to whom that good news has been entrusted. If other men and women are to find the deliverance which we hold so dear, it will only be as God's good news begins to spill over into their lives.

The Church, the Storehouse of God's Good News

There is only one place on earth in which the gospel has taken deep root, and that is the church of Jesus Christ. Individual congregations are local expressions of that universal body which has become the storehouse of the gospel.

This arrangement can be a fragile one at times. As the apostle Paul put it:

> For we preach not ourselves, but Christ Jesus the Lord; and ourselves your servants for Jesus' sake. For God, who commanded the light to shine out of darkness, hath shined in our hearts, to give the light of the knowledge of the glory of God in the face of Jesus Christ. But we have this treasure in earthen vessels (2 Cor. 4:5-7).

Earthen vessels can be most unreliable for conveying a precious cargo from one recipient to the next. Far too many churches and far too many Christians are little more than broken and unreliable vessels in the service of the Lord and the cause of his gospel.

Yet it is precisely at this point that there is such great hope for success. Paul's verse is not yet complete. It continues, "that the excellency of the power may be of God, and not of us."

Knowing the fragility of the human vessels in which his gospel has been deposited, God has determined to accomplish his saving purpose through the church. As Paul elsewhere remarks:

> And hath raised us up together, and made us sit together in heavenly places in Christ Jesus: That in the ages to come he might shew the exceeding riches of his grace in his kindness toward us through Christ Jesus (Eph. 2:6, 7).

In other words, although he has placed his gospel in fragile human vessels to make the good news known, God has not relinquished involvement in the process. He is *with* us, *in* us, and will *through* us proclaim the good news of his grace to a weary generation.

Our task, it would seem, is to understand as fully as possible how we have God's good news as our peculiar possession.

We Have God's Good News Propositionally

By this we mean that the church is able to understand the individual truths which together are the gospel of Jesus Christ. Each of the truths of God's good news— concerning God's grace, man's sin, God's justice and mercy, Jesus' work, and repentance and faith—is a proposition reliable in its own right. At the same time, these truths taken together comprise the gospel of Jesus Christ. The church has been made the guardian of these truths under God's sovereign, superintending care.

This requires of each member of the church a thorough understanding of the good news. It is utterly inexcusable for a believer in Jesus Christ to be unable to explain the gospel to another person. I cannot imagine a businessman being unable to explain his work, or a homemaker incapable of describing her children. In just the same way each Christian ought to be able to explain the gospel that has meant so much in his or her own life.

We have God's good news in propositional form. Our responsibility is to make certain that we fully understand each aspect of that grand message.

We Have God's Good News in Experience

At the same time, the gospel is no mere academic relic. Rather its vitality energizes our daily lives, making all things new and filling us with hope, peace and joy. We have in our own experience evidence of the reality of the gospel. We know whom we have believed, and we are persuaded that he is able to keep us (2 Tim. 1:12).

Paul knew the value of a positive personal experience of Jesus Christ. On several occasions in his own ministry he shared with readers and hearers the blessings which had been worked in his own life through the power of God's good news. He aimed to convince others of its availability for them. The value of a living experience of Jesus Christ was great for Paul, and it can be so for our own work as well.

Do we possess a personal experience of the Lord Jesus Christ? Was there some great fear he has overcome in us? Was there a persistent sin which he has conquered in our lives? Has doubt been vanquished? Have relationships been healed? Has peace gained victory over outward circumstances in our lives?

Each of us should spend time every day meditating on the blessings of the Lord Jesus Christ in our lives. This is the example of the shepherd's psalm (Psalm 23) and many others besides. The certainty of a living experience of Jesus Christ will make our communication of God's good news much more believable and personal.

We Have God's Good News Individually and as a Community

Finally we must see that we possess the gospel of Jesus Christ both as individuals and as a community of those who worship and serve the Creator God. We are many members but one body. Individually we exemplify and proclaim the good news of Jesus' love; corporately we adore him and serve one another in the outworking of his love. In our assemblies his word is declared; in our lives his truths are incarnated. Thus we become living examples of the good news which has been placed within us. We are earthen vessels with an eternal treasure.

There is only one place in this world to which the lost men and women of the world may come to find the good news that can heal their weary souls. Let those who name the name of Jesus Christ prepare to fulfill their calling as witnesses to the men and women of our age.

Review Questions

1. Why does Paul refer to the church as an earthen vessel?
2. What is it that enables that earthen vessel to accomplish its task?
3. What do we mean by propositional truth?
4. What are the main propositional truths which make up the message of the gospel?
5. Why did Paul often share his personal testimony with his readers and hearers?
6. What are the advantages of having a clear and convincing personal testimony concerning your experience of Jesus Christ?
7. How does the church as a body express its possession of the gospel?
8. How do individual believers show that they also have the gospel?

Discussion Questions

1. What is significant about the gospel's being made up of propositional truths? How does that differ from what most people in this relativistic age believe?

2. What are some aspects of your own experience of Jesus Christ that might be meaningful or helpful for others?

3. How might your church begin more effectively to show the rest of your community that it has been made a

storehouse of the gospel?

4. What are some things that might keep individual Christians from fulfilling their calling as God's earthen vessels?

5

How Did We Get God's Good News?

Being a part of the community of those who have received God's good news places awesome responsibilities on each of us. We shall have more to say about this in our next chapter. For now, however, it will be important for us to understand how the good news has come to us through the ages. This in turn will set the stage for a better appreciation of our responsibilities as holders of the gospel in the modern world.

How the Good News Broke upon the World

The good news has not always been with us. Rather, Paul tells us that it was in "the fulness of times" that God determined to declare his good news to the world (Gal. 4:4). When every historical and sociological condition had been adequately prepared and when a sufficient prophetic groundwork had been laid, God sent his only begotten Son to turn aside his wrath. Having accomplished his work, Jesus pronounced it complete and gave up his spirit (John 19:28–30). Three days later he rose from the dead and forty days after that he ascended into heaven. He also provided his disciples with adequate instruction concerning God's kingdom (Acts 1:1-3). He fulfilled the expectations of his Father and set the stage for the spread of God's good news.

On the Day of Pentecost God poured out upon his people the Holy Spirit power for them to be Jesus' witnesses (Acts 1:8). No sooner had the Holy Spirit come upon those faithful men than they set about the task for which they had been called and prepared. Spilling out into the streets of Jerusalem, they all began to tell of "the wonderful works of God" (Acts 2:11).

They established a pattern for all who follow after them in the name of Jesus. Time and again in the New Testament church we see believers testifying to the benefits of God's grace. It was through witnessing that "the Lord added to the church daily such as should be saved" (Acts 2:47). Witnessing by the ordinary people of God continued after Peter and John had been hauled off for a hearing before the authorities (Acts 4:1-4). Unbridled personal evangelism came to be the hallmark of the New Testament church (cf. Acts 19:10; Rom. 1:8; 1 Thess. 1:8).

What Jesus had promised began to be realized by those earliest disciples: "He that believeth on me, as the Scripture hath said, out of his belly shall flow rivers of living water" (John 7:38). Like some fountain opened up, the gospel burst out of the Christian community. Faithful men and women, remembering God's promises and expecting the Spirit to fulfill his work through them, began to reach out to their friends and neighbors with God's good news. Their determination to make the gospel known was uncontrollable, irresistible and roundly effective, establishing churches throughout the Mediterranean basin, churches modeled after the pattern that had its beginnings in Jerusalem. Their example has motivated generations of faithful believers to take the gospel to new lands and peoples.

From the Apostles to the Modern Church

It has now been nearly two thousand years since the gospel first broke upon the world, and we join the earliest Christians in the universal assembly of those who name the name of Jesus Christ. We look forward to rejoicing together in the heavens when our struggle is done and we are home with the Lord in the general assembly of his elect. But until that day we must look to their example to guide our own labors. We must emulate their faithfulness and be effective witnesses to the saving power of our Lord Jesus Christ.

Each of us heard God's good news from another person—a parent, preacher, friend or messenger of grace brought into our lives perhaps for only a moment. Each of those individuals received the gospel in a similar manner. There is an unbroken chain of faithful witnesses reaching all the way back to the earliest days of the church. Through the persistence of the believing community the gospel has come to be *our* treasure in earthen vessels. Here is how the apostle Paul saw this process of men and women coming to faith in Christ:

> For whosoever shall call upon the name of the Lord shall be saved. How then shall they call on him in whom they have not believed? and how shall they believe in him of

whom they have not heard? and how shall they hear
without a preacher? (Rom. 10:13, 14)

This truth is taken too lightly in our day. The gospel
has not come down to us without cost. Often it has required courage and risks to take the gospel from one nation or one generation to the next. At times it has required the church to "go underground," protecting the
treasure through secret meetings.

The history of Christian missions and outreach is filled
with examples of courage, boldness, suffering, perseverance and collaboration to ensure the transmission of the
gospel. We stand at the end of that line of transmission.
We are the ones for whom the saints and martyrs of the
past gave their lives and fortunes. What a tragedy it
would be if we should fail to accept the responsibility of
passing the good news on to the generations to come.

So Great a Cloud of Witnesses

The writer of the book of Hebrews was acutely aware
of his responsibility in the light of the sufferings and
faithfulness of previous generations of witnesses. After
cataloguing the strivings and persistence of his ancestors
in the faith he wrote to his readers these words:

> Wherefore seeing we also are compassed about with so
> great a cloud of witnesses, let us lay aside every weight,
> and the sin which doth so easily beset us, and let us run
> with patience the race that is set before us (Heb. 12:1).

It is to a fuller understanding of that race, and particularly of its preaching mandate, that we shall turn our
attention next.

Review Questions

1. What is promised in Jesus' words in Acts 1:8?
2. How did that promise begin to show itself in the lives of those first Christians?
3. How did their lives become a pattern for other believers to follow?
4. What is the significance of Jesus' remark about the "rivers of living water"?
5. How does Paul say that men and women come to call on the name of the Lord?
6. How should the example of previous generations of believers affect us?
7. If the transmission of the gospel is to continue into the future what will be required of this present generation of believers?

Discussion Questions

1. Take some time now, either privately or in small groups, to practice going over the outline of the gospel that was given in chapter 1. By now you should have that outline fairly well memorized, so try saying it as conversationally as possible, rather than in a merely rote fashion.

2. Put yourself in the place of those first Christians in Acts 2. The Holy Spirit has come; you have rushed into the streets; you come up excitedly to the first person you meet; and what is it that you begin to say? How do you get started telling him what you want to share?

3. Talk about some of the responses those early Christians were likely to have encountered. Can you cite some instances in the New Testament to indicate how their message was received?

4. Can you think of any outstanding witnesses from past ages? What about them comes to mind? Is there any link between their faithful preaching and our situation today? The following names might serve to jog your memory:

–Augustine	–Calvin	–H. Taylor
–Boniface	–Knox	–C. T. Studd
–Wycliffe	–Carey	–M. Slessor
–Luther	–Livingstone	–A. Carmichael

6

What Are We to Do with God's Good News?

It is no small matter to be the community which has been entrusted with God's good news. The responsibility of bearing the gospel in our day transfers to each of us who carries the name of Jesus Christ.

From the beginning it has been God's intention to have his will declared to all. Within God's will all find their greatest peace and happiness. The task that falls to us today as earthen vessels for the gospel remains essentially the same as that of our ancestors in the faith—making God's good news known. In this chapter we want to place our responsibility for communicating the gospel within the larger context of God's plan as spelled out in the Scriptures.

God's Original Intention

From the beginning God has intended that human beings should be the means through which his will is carried out on earth. On the day he was created man was given a commission by God which has never been revoked. He was to subdue the earth, to fill it with seed like himself (at that time, without sin and in fellowship with God) and to exercise dominion over the whole of creation that would reflect the good purposes of God. Man was to take his example from the creative handiwork of God himself who, on the sixth day of creation, pronounced the earth and all things in it "very good" (Gen. 1:26–31).

Had this design been carried out according to the mandate of God the whole human race would have known no obstacle of sin between them and their Creator. Moreover their work—as well as their homes, personal relationships and every other aspect of their lives—would have continued to carry the stamp of divine approval.

This original mandate was interrupted by the entrance of sin into human life. Nevertheless God was not to be deterred from his original design. He determined that people and nations should still come to know him and to benefit from the relationship with himself into which he would bring them by his grace.

A Further Elaboration

Thus it was that, years later, God chose a man through whom a new race of people would be initiated and out of whose loins a deliverer would one day come to complete the heavenly plan. In Genesis 12:1–3 God gave to Abram the vision of what he intended to do in and through this new people. All the earth was to be blessed as the people of God multiplied and became a channel of good to all. They were to be a watershed for the nations. Some people would protect, provide for and bless them and thus find a refuge under the shelter of the same covenant that guided the people of God. Others would curse and renounce them, thus dooming themselves to perpetual divine displeasure.

The mandate to multiply as a people under God and to seek to bring good to the nations continued unabated. Moreover a promise was given to the people that they would be a source of blessing to all nations, that something would occur within them as a people that would overflow all tribes and peoples.

Thus instructed, Abraham became the father of a people who for two millenia were guided by the promises and covenant of God. Through the patriarchs—Moses, Joshua, Samuel, David and all the prophets—the memory of God's mandate and the lure of his promise drove them onward seeking to realize his plan of redemption and fulfillment. Isaiah was told to look ahead to a day when the people of God would serve as a focal point to which all the nations would be drawn (Is. 2:1–5). It was in the midst of the people of God that God's ways were to be learned, fellowship with him was to be found and power to renounce all human hostilities was to be claimed. Driven by this vision our ancestors in the faith endured hardships and undertook courageous ventures to show their faith, undergirded as it was by God's promises (cf. Heb. 11). It is this cloud of witnesses that looks down on us, the current community of earthen vessels, the latest generation to have received the mandate and promise that have motivated the people of God in every age.

How God Will Draw Them

Ours is an age teeming with problems and trials. We might be tempted to think that there are greater needs and more pressing demands upon our time and resources than the communication of God's good news. Such a belief requires further examination.

The Lord Jesus Christ came into a world very much like our own. It was a world torn with human depravity and the disparity of classes and nations. It was a world held under by oppression, one in which exploitation and intimidation were the norm for the rich and privileged. Families were in turmoil, freedom was a rare commodity and the lives of women and children were negotiable entities at best.

As Jesus looked out on the needs of his day he considered how best to address the suffering and hardship that he encountered on every hand. His message to his followers makes it very clear what he saw as the most significant undertaking to which they could commit themselves:

> Go ye therefore, and teach all nations, baptizing them in the name of the Father, and of the Son, and of the Holy Ghost: Teaching them to observe all things whatsoever I have commanded you: and, lo, I am with you alway, even unto the end of the world (Matt. 28:19, 20).

Evidently Jesus was convinced that the plan of God must go on. The mandate to make God's good news known as the first step in bringing his blessings to all must not be interrupted by immediate temporal concerns, be they ever so urgent.

This mandate remains for us. As those who have received God's good news and who now serve as its earthen vessels, we must not fail to follow in the footsteps of our forebears. We must continue the faithful tradition of declaring the gospel to the nations, of holding up for their consideration the promises and mandates of God their Creator.

In Revelation 3:14–16 Jesus, the Faithful Witness, sent a letter to an early Christian church urging them to take up their responsibility to make disciples. That same charge remains for each one of us. We must harken to his words and rally to the cause for which we have been recreated in him.

Let us resolve then to take up the mantle of those who have preceded us in the faith. Let us, like them, harken to God's mandate and concentrate on his promise so that we might be found faithful in the task of making God's good news known.

Review Questions

1. What things are included in God's original mandate as it is given in Genesis 1:26-28?

2. In what ways is the mandate given to Abram in Genesis 12:1-3 merely a restating of that original mandate?

3. What is the lesson summarized for us in Hebrews 11?

4. Why do you suppose Matthew 28:18-20 is so often referred to as "the Great Commission"?

5. Whose responsibility is it to carry out the Great Commission?

Discussion Questions

1. Think of a church you have known which has let the light of the gospel fail. What are the consequences over time for such a church? What are the consequences for the community or the nation in which such churches are found?

2. How is it, do you suppose, that churches come to lose their zeal for the gospel? How can that zeal be rekindled?

3. Discuss the role of each of the following in helping a church to find its place among God's faithful witnesses:
   -Pastor
   -Officers
   -Laymen and women

4. What are the greatest obstacles currently standing in

the way of *your* church becoming a more faithful witnessing community? Of *your* becoming a more consistent witness?

7

How Can I Learn to Share God's Good News?

By now there should be no doubt in the reader's mind concerning our need to begin making God's good news known to the men and women in our generation. Nobody else is going to undertake this for us; the lost people of this world are not likely to stumble upon the gospel; the mandate of Scripture and the heritage of the people of God weigh heavily upon us. We must not fail to take up the task of the Great Commission in our own relationships and acquaintances.

Happily this is a challenge to which, by the power of God's Holy Spirit, we can rise. We can become effective witnesses to Jesus Christ. We can know the joy and the thrill of being used of God to lead others to Christ. All that is required of us is that we be willing to take the time and venture the faith that this requires. It is to these matters that we turn our attention in this chapter.

God's Good News Reviewed

Let's take a moment to review the outline of the gospel

that we have been learning throughout this study. This time, however, we will bring in some Scripture references to bolster the points we want to emphasize:

GRACE
- Eternal life is a free gift, Eph. 2:8.
- It is not earned or deserved, Eph. 2:9.

MAN
- Man is a sinner, Rom. 3:23.
- He cannot save himself, Prov. 14:12.

GOD
- God is merciful, 1 John 4:8.
- God is just and must punish sin, Ex. 34:7.

CHRIST
- He is the infinite, eternal God/Man, Jn. 1:1, 14.
- He came to die on a cross and purchase a place for us in heaven, Rom. 6:23.

FAITH
- Faith is the key to heaven, Rom. 1:17.
- It is not mere intellectual belief or temporal faith, but trusting in Jesus Christ alone for salvation, Acts 16:31.

This simple outline provides a starting point for developing a conversational presentation of the gospel that can be shared in any situation, any context, with any sort of person. The more you practice sharing this message, the more you work at making it personal and conversational, and the more you work at developing new relationships with the men and women around you, the more effective you will become at making God's good news known to them.

Certainly such facility will not come naturally, nor will you have acquired it merely by memorizing a rote outline. Becoming an effective witness to Jesus Christ requires prayerful and faithful learning and practice, studying to show yourself approved to God, a workman who has no need to be ashamed of the gospel (2 Tim. 2:15).

Familiarity to Spontaneity

Jesus taught us to believe that we could become effective witnesses for him. Indeed he encouraged us to believe that bearing effective witness for him would become the spontaneous outgrowth of our developing relationship with him. Here is the way he put it in John 7:38:

> He that believeth on me, as the scripture hath said, out of his belly shall flow rivers of living water.

Such Christlike witnessing does not come automatically. Instead we *grow* into becoming effective witnesses—being changed, as Paul put it, from one experience of Christ living through us to the next under the guiding power of the Holy Spirit (2 Cor. 3:18).

Such spontaneity in bearing witness for our Lord Jesus is the goal. We must begin somewhere in achieving that objective. For some of us it will mean that we must practice the message over and over to ourselves, to members of our family and to other believing friends willing to permit us to rehearse our presentation. Practicing the message of the gospel will enable us to attain a familiarity with its contents that will help us personalize the gospel. Early believers often shared with each other the glorious message and how grace had affected their lives. Our determination to become effective witnesses for Jesus Christ can also catalyze the sharing of God's grace among fellow church members.

The Faith to Try God's Power

The real test of becoming effective witnesses to Jesus Christ will come as we begin to reach out to our neighbors with the message of the gospel. Any conversation, any discussion and any situation can be used for initiating a presentation. If we have personalized our presentation, practiced it and are sensitive to the interests and needs of our neighbors, we can become skilled at sharing the gospel with them.

The biggest problem that we can expect to encounter will be getting started. Getting started in a presentation of the gospel is a matter of alertness and faith.

We must be alert to opportunities to tell others about the gospel. Very often their needs, their hurts and their joys can serve as door-openers for sharing something which has meaning for us. We do not need to use undue pressure nor do we need to feel that we must race through the complete presentation on the first try. Rather we must be alert to the leading of the Spirit of God as he opens avenues of witnessing.

We must also believe in the availability of his power to complete the work which has been begun in us. Jesus promised that when the Holy Spirit came we would receive power to bear witness for him (Acts 1:8). Do we really believe that? When the opportunity to begin sharing our faith presents itself do we fall back on the power of the Holy Spirit to enable us to share our faith in a clear and meaningful way?

Certainly the teaching of Scripture is that we should. Faith to bear witness is like a muscle: the more it is exercised the more it grows and becomes powerful. As Jim Kennedy once put it, "The more you evangelize, the more you evangelize." Conversely, when you neglect to use this great muscle of faith it begins to atrophy and your witness for Christ becomes ineffective if not non-existent.

Thus we must put what we have learned to use in our everyday lives. We must reach out to others with the gospel, calling them to hear the word of God and to look to him in faith.

A Promise Worth Claiming

In John 14:12 Jesus made a promise which is so astonishing and so germane to the question before us that it is well worth recalling here:

> Verily, verily, I say unto you, He that believeth on me, the works that I do shall he do also; and greater works than these shall he do; because I go unto my Father.

In going to the Father Jesus knew he would be giving

his Spirit to the church. And his Spirit would empower us to become vibrant and effective witnesses for Christ that, as was the case in the early church, could turn the world upside down (Acts 17:6).

This is a challenge and a calling to which each of us in the body of Christ must—and can!—rise.

HOW CAN I LEARN TO SHARE GOD'S GOOD NEWS?

Review Questions

1. To which part of the gospel outline do each of the following verses apply:

   Rom. 3:23   John 1:1, 14
   1 John 4:8b   Prov. 14:12
   Rom. 6:23   Acts 16:31

2. What does Jesus promise in John 7:38? Can we expect this to come automatically?

3. What is the significance of 2 Cor. 3:18 for learning to share our faith in Christ?

4. What is promised in Acts 1:8 to help us in our witnessing?

5. What two things are required for us to get started sharing our faith with another person?

6. How does John 14:12 apply to our witnessing?

Discussion Questions

1. Take some time to practice sharing the outline of the gospel you have been learning with another person. Try to incorporate some of the Scripture verses into the presentation. You can do this by stating the truth to be shared and then saying, "As the Bible says, . . ." You do not need to cite the reference.

2. In what ways do you suppose the early believers turned the world upside down? How was their witnessing related to this?

3. How does the gospel turn a community upside down?

What changes start coming into a person's life when he becomes a true believer in Christ? In the light of this what is the only reasonable place to begin in making this a better world?

8

How Can I Get Them Interested in God's Good News?

Preparing yourself to share God's good news in daily relationships is just the first step in developing a witnessing way of life. Spontaneous evangelism—witnessing that wells up from within and reaches out in the power of the Holy Spirit—can become a prominent feature of our lives. We must be faithful in understanding the gospel, in rehearsing to one another its benefits and in looking to God for the boldness which effective evangelism requires.

Sharing God's good news with others involves a process of communication. It requires those who would employ that process to understand it as fully as possible to be able to use it with maximum effect.

The early Christians were not ignorant of the subtleties of effective communication. Knowing that they had the most significant message that anyone could ever hear, the apostles and their disciples took care to reach their neighbors in a manner and at a level which helped to ensure that their message would receive a fair hearing. In their approach to the people of their age we can find insight to help us in getting the attention of our neighbors.

The Responsibility to Understand

In Acts 17 we get a look at the apostle Paul preparing to witness in Athens and then approaching unbelievers with the message of the gospel. His *modus operandi* can be instructive for us in our evangelism.

Notice that Paul's first approach to witness in Athens was to understand as much as possible about the people to whom he would be speaking. Paul took the time to look around the city (vs. 16) until he was sufficiently familiar with it and its people to develop a proper burden for them in their lostness. How did he do this?

Paul's most effective way of learning to understand others seems to have been simply to move around among them. Paul mingled with the Athenians (vs. 17) in some of the common places to which they resorted. We cannot develop an understanding of people without spending time among them—in their homes, over lunch or coffee, in the midst of their trials and successes, in the places where they take their recreation. This does not mean that we will join them in sinful practices; rather it means that we will not allow ourselves to become so isolated from the lost men and women around us that we become out-of-touch with their world.

Church growth experts talk about a principle of lift which comes into play in the Christian life. By this they mean that the longer one is a Christian the more he is lifted out of the world. Relationships become more and more with Christians alone; time is spent increasingly in the work of the church; interests follow a course of Christian growth and development, often causing the believer to leave the cares and concerns of the world—and the people in it—behind.

Effective evangelists for Christ must fight the principle of lift by working to stay in touch with those around us so as to understand them and their world. Only thus will we be effective in bearing witness to them.

Paul had also taken the time to familiarize himself with the Athenian world through formal study. His familiarity with Greek philosophy and poetry—not to mention the Greek language—bears testimony to hours of prayerful and reflective study in books and classes.

Here again we as Christians need to take care that our study is not exclusively centered around spiritual matters. As crucial as these are for Christian growth and development we need to spend a portion of our time understanding the issues and events which occupy the thinking of those to whom we hope to proclaim Christ.

If we are to be effective in evangelism we shall need to rethink our understanding of those around us. By spending time with them and taking the time to stay in touch with what is going on in their world we will, like Paul, be able to develop and sustain a genuine sense of concern for them in their lostness. This concern will constrain us to share our faith as the Lord gives us opportunity.

Talking Their Language

Once we have begun to develop a proper understanding of the needs and interests of our neighbors we will be able to start talking to them about the gospel in an intelligent and relevant manner. A couple of other points from the ministry of Paul in Athens deserve our attention at this point.

First, notice Paul's nonjudgmental attitude toward his new neighbors. When he first began speaking to them in verse 22 Paul did not condemn them for their sin and idolatry. Instead he looked for a positive starting point. He was interested in their listening to what he had to say, not in their throwing up defenses against him and his message. Paul began sharing on a positive note with what might be seen as a compliment to the Athenians on the seriousness with which they approached religion.

In beginning to share with our neighbors this is a wise principle to learn. There is so much of a positive nature in the lives of those around us if only we will look for it. Our neighbors will be much more likely to listen to us and discuss with us if they perceive that we appreciate the good things in their lives. This principle of nonjudgmentalism and looking for a positive starting point is one of the most important aspects of effective evangelism that any of us can learn. By using it effectively we can ensure that even if our message is rejected over and over again our neighbors will always be willing and eager to talk with us another time.

Second, notice that Paul also was careful to employ concepts and ideas to which his audience would readily relate. In verse 28 Paul uses quotes from two Greek philosophers to make his point about our being made in the image of God. His audience understood him fully.

So we too need to make certain that our sharing is filled more with the images from our culture than the jargon of theology and the church. Why should we waste our time using terms like "redeemed" and "saved" when concepts such as "forgiveness," "wholeness" and "everlasting life" can convey so much more? And why should we dwell on the "infilling of the Spirit" when our lost friend is looking for a purpose to fill up his life or a bond to patch up a crumbling marriage?

Effective evangelism means sharing the gospel in a manner and at a level that gets the message across so that our neighbor can clearly understand the eternal significance of what we have to say. It is our responsibility to develop these skills.

Telling the Message Straight

At some point in our sharing we will need to move from casual conversation to communicating the good news of Jesus Christ. As we begin to do this we must make certain that we mince no words when it comes to what Christ has done and what God requires.

Very often the temptation may come to try to accommodate our message to the situation as we know it in the life of our neighbor. If he is a good churchgoer we may, out of love, be tempted to confirm his churchgoing as what God requires. Or if our friend is a particularly good person (in the world's eyes) we may feel inclined to give the impression that God receives him on the basis of his works rather than Christ's. Paul was very careful to let the Athenians know that only in Jesus Christ was there hope of escaping the judging wrath of God (cf. vs. 31). Just so, out of true love for our lost friends, must we be careful to tell them straight out what is expected of them in coming to faith in Christ. We shall have more to say about this in our next chapter.

We can learn to share God's good news in a manner that will help to ensure that our friends and neighbors will be willing to listen. The lessons from Paul's ministry in Athens need to be contemplated and practiced over and over again until they are effectively internalized and become part of our witnessing way of life.

Review Questions

1. What do we learn about effective communications from Acts 17:16?
2. How was Paul able to develop a genuine concern for the Athenians in their lostness?
3. What does Acts 17:17 teach us about learning to understand the people around us? What about Acts 17:28?
4. What do we mean by the principle of lift?
5. Explain the principle of nonjudgmentalism and the positive starting point.
6. What do we mean when we warn against the improper use of theological and church jargon?
7. What is a major temptation which often confronts us in witnessing to people that we have come to know and understand?

Discussion Questions

1. What are some ways that you can get to know the people around you better?

2. What are some of the pressing personal issues that we might expect to find on the minds of our neighbors and friends? Does the gospel have a word of comfort or consolation for any of these matters?

3. What are some contemporary issues and problems which would seem to be directly related to modern man's need for the gospel?

4. Take some time now to share with someone else the outline of the gospel as you have been learning it. Be sure to do this in a conversational manner.

9

What Do We Need to Tell Them about God's Good News?

We know what we want to say to our neighbors concerning God's good news and we have begun to discover how we can make that news interesting and relevant for them. We have already put in place the most essential building blocks of an effective, witnessing way of life.

In this chapter we need to take a closer look at particular aspects of the gospel that we will want to make very clear. It will not be possible for our neighbors to make a proper response to the message without understanding the matters which we are about to consider. We must take extra care to make certain that our communication of the gospel clearly includes what follows.

The Gospel Is Historically True

To us it may seem rather insignificant and unimportant to have to emphasize that the events which constitute the heart and core of the gospel are historically true. Nevertheless many of our friends and neighbors have for one reason or another come to regard the life, death and resurrection of Jesus Christ as interesting, even beautiful, but hardly the sort of stuff that takes place in our stream of history.

People in the modern world have been led to believe that religion is a mythical attempt to explain the phenomena of everyday life and the world. Many of our neighbors may be willing to acknowledge the right of each individual to choose his or her own myths, yet they understand these myths to be more the stuff of psychological necessity than historical reality. For people to respond to the gospel on this basis is to trivialize the message and to neutralize its power to transform human lives. The secular tendencies of our day require that we emphasize that the gospel is really true and that the events it reports actually took place in the same time/space continuum in which we currently exist.

There has also been a trend in contemporary Christianity that has relegated the events of the gospel to a level of history that exists only in the mind of faith. The story of the gospel becomes something in a realm of "faith history" within the subjective experience of men and women. No person who has this kind of understanding of the events of the cross and the empty tomb will be able to make the kind of self-conscious response that the gospel requires.

Finally, the popularity of the gospel may lead some to respond favorably before the radical implications of the gospel have had a chance to sink in. By helping them to see that we are calling them to an acceptance of historical events and not just to join the latest sociological trend we may be able to preclude some premature and inauthentic professions of faith.

Like Peter we need to make certain that those to whom we are witnessing clearly understand that we are not following cleverly invented stories (2 Pet. 1:16). The significance of our message—as well as of its promises and demands—will be in focus for our neighbors if we are careful to communicate the historicity of the gospel to them in no uncertain terms.

The Promise of a Meaningful and Powerful Life

The gospel of Jesus Christ must not be set forth like pronouncements which come from governments or public officials. These are conveyed with much solemnity and pomp yet their practical implications for our everyday lives are often nonexistent. We listen with interest and applaud politely, then we go on our ways completely unaffected, shortly to forget what was announced.

Unlike the announcments of public officials the gospel is filled with significance for human life. It is to be set forth clearly, excitedly, personally and with its promise of new life held out like a gem for the unbeliever to consider.

Ours is an age virtually devoid of abiding meaning for human life. Men and women ricochet like pinballs from one job, relationship or fad to the next in a desperate attempt to find genuine meaning. Yet people, work and avocations are all temporal and soon lose their allure. They are shortly seeking more enduring meaning once again.

And it is precisely this that God's good news provides.

Jesus said that he had come to give life and to give it abundantly (John 10:10). He talked about being "the way, the truth, and the life" (John 14:6). His followers came to realize that he alone was really worth living for. They learned to live to the fullest in his service.

Jesus is the one who gives meaning and purpose even to the most mundane facets of our daily lives. He enriches our relationships and energizes our time on the job. He opens up vistas of truth and beauty that never existed before. He creates sympathy and love and fills us with power to care for and serve others in his name. Because he has redeemed the world and brought the wisdom and power of God to bear upon the whole of human life he is able to infuse our experience with purpose that can never be revoked.

It is this breadth of meaning, this fount of power for living, that needs to be displayed before unbelievers. Only such bold and confident witnessing to Jesus Christ will convince our purposeless age of the significance of our message.

The Need for a Self-conscious Response

The gospel is not the sort of news to which people can respond merely by saying, "That's nice," or "That's interesting." There are life and death matters at stake in accepting or rejecting God's good news. Eternal destinies will be confirmed in the responses which our neighbors make. It is our responsibility to help our friends see that they must weigh carefully the matters that we have set before them. They must be fully conscious of the consequences of their decision.

In our next chapter we will consider the various responses that are likely to be forthcoming. Here we want to discuss the various aspects of a proper response to the message.

First, we need to make certain that our neighbors know that a proper response is wholehearted. The gospel is not calling them merely to a guarantee against the terrors of hell. Jesus is not to be received only as Savior. Paul tells us that he reigns as Lord (Phil. 2:9-11). They must be willing to acknowledge his lordship over the whole of their lives.

Too often in evangelical circles we give the impression that praying a simple prayer of confession and asking Jesus "to come into our hearts" is a proper response to the gospel. Once that has been nailed down (the impression is often given) all is well in the new convert's life.

Yet such is not the case. Unless men and women are willing to come to Jesus on the only terms that he is willing to accept he will not heed their shallow professions at all. We must be careful to say that this incredible good news, which holds out such promise and such power, is available only to those who acknowledge its claims upon the whole of their lives.

This means, in the second place, that they have to repent of their sins. This will involve both initial repentance and an ongoing vigilance, looking to God's Spirit to lead them into repentance from whatever sins may appear from time to time. If a basic attitude of repentance is not apparent then it is doubtful that your neighbor is willing truly to accept the gospel, for he will yet be hoarding some nook or cranny of daily life for his own lordship. Christ is not willing to compete with our petty claims to lordship over this or that area of experience. He demands total allegiance, and only a commitment to ongoing repentance will properly acknowledge his claims.

Finally, we need to help them understand the true nature of saving faith. Faith in Jesus Christ involves a genuine transfer of our trust for eternal life from anything other than Christ to Christ alone. As the old hymn makes clear, "Nothing in my hand I bring, Simply to thy cross I cling." Faith is looking to Jesus Christ alone for the gift of eternal life.

This faith *can* be expressed in a prayer of acceptance, although it need not be. However, leading your neighbor in a brief prayer acknowledging his or her need of Christ and receiving him as Savior and Lord can provide a helpful starting point for a new life of faith.

We must be careful to make clear these three critical matters. Our witnessing will be much more powerful, and positive responses to our witnessing will be much more genuine and lasting, when we have persisted in emphasizing the matters we have discussed.

Review Questions

1. What has our secular age done to affect the attitudes of many people concerning the events of the gospel?

2. What is the significance of 2 Pet. 1:16 for our witnessing?

3. What do we mean when we say that Jesus came to give an abundant life to men?

4. Why is it important to show that the gospel brings meaning and power to the whole of life?

5. What is involved in a wholehearted response to the gospel?

6. Why can leading your friend in a prayer of faith be helpful?

Discussion Questions

1. Put yourself in the shoes of an unbeliever you might know. How does such a person view your religious faith? What is the nature of your belief in God as he sees it? How does this relate to the historicity of the gospel?

2. Discuss some ways in which the gospel has brought new meaning or new power to some aspect of your own life. How might you incorporate this into your presentation of the gospel? At which of the points of the gospel outline might you share it?

3. What are some problems that might result from failing to make clear what a proper response to the gospel should be?

4. What might be the elements of a brief prayer of faith such as you might lead your neighbor in saying as he receives Christ?

5. Take some time now to practice with another person your presentation of the gospel.

10

How Will They Respond to God's Good News?

The gospel is designed to make an impact on people. God's good news is not like any other piece of news or information that people may encounter. The gospel proclaims that God has forgiven sin through the person and work of Jesus Christ. It sets forth the claims of God on the lives of men and women, calling them to repent and believe his good news. They cannot and must not be expected to remain indifferent to what they hear from us. Instead the people to whom we bear witness about the risen Lord Jesus Christ can be expected to respond in some very definite, even predictable, ways.

Our responsibility is to understand what we might expect and be prepared to take the next step with our neighbors. In this chapter we will look at some typical responses to the gospel and consider some reasonable procedures for following up those to whom we have witnessed, regardless of their response.

Three Types of Response

In Acts 17:32-34 we are given an overview of the kinds of responses to our witnessing that we can expect:

> And when they heard of the resurrection of the dead, some mocked: and others said, We will hear thee again of this matter. So Paul departed from among them. Howbeit certain men clave unto him, and believed.

The first type of response after Paul's public witness to the Lord Jesus Christ we might categorize as rejection of what was preached: some sneered. We must expect that some of our neighbors will be unimpressed by the gospel and will tell us outright that they are not interested. Included in this group will be those who may become angry, even to the point of being insulting. What are we to make of this?

Such responses need not surprise us. After all, Jesus was regularly confronted by mockers, scoffers and those who sought to do him ill. The early apostles were all subjected to the same kind of rejection, even persecution, for their testimony concerning Jesus. The Lord himself told us to expect that we would be hated because of the gospel (Matt. 10:22).

Jesus made it clear to his disciples that those who came right out and welcomed the good news would be a small minority (Matt. 7:14). Thus it should not catch us off guard if some respond to us in a manner such as that which Paul encountered among the Athenians.

At the same time we need to do everything in our power to make certain that when we are rejected by our

neighbors it is because of the gospel and not because of
our manners. We shall have more to say about this in a
later chapter.

The second response that we can expect is also clear:
others said they wanted to hear Paul again on the subject.
Some will not reject what we have proclaimed but neither
will they be prepared to make a profession of faith in the
Lord Jesus. These people may be described as being "not
far from the kingdom" (Mark 12:34). All that remains to
be discovered is whether they are tending toward Jesus or
away from him.

For our part we need to be careful that we do not make
the mistake of assuming that, since they were not willing
to accept the gospel at this particular time, they have
therefore forever rejected it. We will need to be prepared
to accommodate their request for further discussions
while respecting their freedom to choose and their individual responsibility before God.

It is the final response that interests us most: a few men
became followers of Paul and believed. We must expect
some of our neighbors to be ready to come to Christ in
humble repentance and faith after we have clearly made
known the gospel. Those whom God has determined to
draw to himself will come irresistibly, unhesitatingly and
often emotionally as the Holy Spirit applies the saving
work of God and brings them to faith (John 6:44, 63).
This is a time for great rejoicing, thanking and praising
God. There is no human joy quite like that of being used
by God to lead another person to Christ. It is a privilege
to which each of us has been called and one that we must
all seek to embrace. God will be faithful in using us in his

saving work to the extent that we are faithful and available to be used (2 Tim. 2:2).

Regardless of how our neighbors respond to God's good news we need to be prepared to take the next step. Let's look at some reasonable strategies for following up our initial witnessing encounter.

Follow-up

The place to begin following up your witnessing contact is prayer. It takes God to move the hearts of men and women, and it also takes God's Spirit to convince the newly saved that they have a secure and eternal home with the Father. No matter how our neighbors respond to our witness we must pray for them faithfully, entrusting them to God's care and beseeching him that his mercy may penetrate the deepest recesses of their lives.

I have often found it helpful from time to time to tell a neighbor or acquaintance that I was praying for him on a regular basis and to ask if he had any specific requests or needs. This may be all it takes to open the door. It may provide for another opportunity to share Jesus. At the very least it expresses genuine Christian concern—and it also keeps those who have rejected the gospel mindful that a sovereign God is keeping an eye on them.

Besides prayer, literature can be a helpful tool for follow-up in a witnessing situation—a copy of the Gospel of John is excellent for this. You might ask your neighbor to read it over, maybe one chapter a day for the next week. You should promise to get back to him to see if he has any questions.

Other literature can be helpful: there are tracts, booklets and leaflets which present the gospel, portions of Scripture or helpful Christian testimonies which can be left for your neighbor to read at his leisure. For those who come to faith in Christ such literature can remind them of the commitment they have made.

Inviting your neighbor to church with you (I emphasize the *with you* part) can also be an effective follow-up device. Because he knows you your neighbor will feel more comfortable in the presence of strangers if he is with you. Even those who reject the gospel ought at least to make sure that they know what they are casting aside. Inviting them to church can help them to hear God's good news from another angle.

Especially will you want to encourage those who come to faith in Jesus to begin attending church. Help them get into a Bible study where they can learn about the importance of the word of God and how to read and study it, prayer, worship and the fellowship of believers. Take new believers with you to your own church activities, always introducing them to others as your friend, not as a new believer.

Finally, making yourself available to new relationships with others can be helpful. We read that "Paul departed from them," but that was because of the special nature of his traveling ministry. Elsewhere he encourages us to stay in touch with unbelievers, developing relationships to provide conversational contexts for future testimony to the grace of God (cf. 1 Cor. 5:9, 10). We must become "living letters" for our neighbors, flesh-and-blood examples of what we have claimed concerning the transforming power of the gospel (2 Cor. 3:2). We shall have more to say about this shortly.

Those with whom we share the treasure of the gospel will certainly respond. By understanding what those responses are likely to be we will be better prepared to follow up and help our neighbors gain further understanding of God's good news.

Review Questions

1. What three types of responses to the gospel are mentioned in Acts 17:32-34?
2. Why should we not be surprised when certain people reject the gospel?
3. What takes place when a person comes to saving faith as a result of our witness?
4. Why is prayer an important part of follow-up?
5. Explain how to use literature in following up a witnessing situation.
6. What are some important things to keep in mind about helping your neighbor come to church?
7. Why is developing new relationships an important part of effective follow-up?

Discussion Questions

1. Take some time now to make a conversational presentation of the gospel outline you have learned in the course of this study.

2. What are some attitudes you might express or some actions you might perform that could create a hostile response to the gospel?

3. What are some workable ways of going about developing relationships with those who do not receive the gospel, especially those who do not reject it?

4. What are some activities in your own church that

might be good for bringing in a new believer?

5. Can you think of any other approaches to follow-up that might be useful for helping to stay in touch with a person who did not receive the gospel?

11

What Is God's Good-News Way of Life?

One of the mistakes that evangelistic Christians and churches frequently make is believing that their witnessing responsibilities can be fulfilled by a sophisticated or carefully organized program of evangelism in the local church. As helpful and effective as such ministries can be they do not include all that the New Testament requires of us as witnesses for Jesus Christ.

We need to see our witnessing as a way of life, a lifestyle that infiltrates normal relationships and flows into our conversations naturally and spontaneously—Jesus living out his witness through us. This is precisely what can begin to take place. As the apostle Paul put it,

> I am crucified with Christ: nevertheless I live; yet not I, but Christ liveth in me: and the life which I now live in the flesh I live by the faith of the Son of God, who loved me, and gave himself for me (Gal 2:20).

Doing and Being

Let's look carefully at a verse of Scripture:

> But ye shall receive power, after that the Holy Ghost is come upon you: and ye shall be witnesses unto me both

in Jerusalem, and in all Judea, and in Samaria, and unto the uttermost part of the earth (Acts 1:8).

The most important word in this verse as far as a witnessing way of life is concerned is the Greek verb *esesthe*. This word is translated in English "ye shall be." The author is saying something significant about our existence in this world as witnesses. Jesus wants us to understand that our evangelistic responsibilities are not satisfied merely by doing evangelism. Rather we are to *be* witnesses to him, to have a quality of life, a being-in-the-world that *in every aspect* bears testimony to our commitment to Jesus Christ. We are not just to "do evangelism" or "go witnessing." We are to *be* witnesses.

What does this mean, and how may we begin to address this challenge?

Being Witnesses for Christ

The witnessing way of life involves total commitment that submits every aspect of one's life to Jesus Christ. In a real sense it involves losing our own distinct existence and taking up the life which is bestowed by Jesus Christ on each of us. Jesus put it this way:

If any man will come after me, let him deny himself, and take up his cross, and follow me. For whosoever will save his life shall lose it: and whosoever will lose his life for my sake shall find it (Matt. 16:24, 25).

Nothing short of a life surrendered to the purposes and will of our Lord will suffice. We must look more closely to see just what this involves.

In the first place, a witnessing way of life will encompass our outlook on life. In the way we understand the world and the people in it, in the ideas we entertain, in the aspirations we hold for ourselves and in our thought processes, we are to let the mind of Christ and the purposes of the gospel serve as the final filter for our thinking. We are daily—even hourly—to be renewed in the spirit of our minds and to put on the new self (Eph. 4:20-24). We are to take every thought which enters our minds captive to the obedience of Jesus Christ (2 Cor. 10:5).

This outlook of submission to the mind of Christ will require earnest prayer, thorough study and hearty encouragement of one another if it is to become a way of life. Yet once it begins to permeate our outlook on life the rest of our lives will begin to come into line. The place to begin in developing a witnessing way of life is in our thinking about our lives. As we are renewed in our minds we will lay aside our former manner of living and begin more and more to put on the new self that is being re-created into the likeness of Jesus Christ (2 Cor. 3:18).

This will involve us in new patterns of living. Everything we do, every choice and decision, will be affected by our outlook. Our lives will display our thinking. Our relationships will begin to show the dignity and worth we give to others and the love we are learning for them. Our work will reflect our desire to serve God with our hands. It will display the creativity and excellence for which we were created. We will use possessions as trusts from the Lord to serve his purposes. This will change the use we make of our homes, the types of purchases we make, the level of lifestyle we choose and the liberality of our giving.

This way of life will support the testimony of one who claims allegiance to a God of love and grace. Only such a renewed manner of living will support the credibility of our spoken witness for Jesus Christ. Where it is present our witness will be believable; where it is absent our hypocrisy will undermine the truth of what we have to say.

Finally, a witnessing way of life will take every opportunity for declaring God's good news. Paul says that as the Lord leads us we ought to speak boldly (Eph. 6:20). As we yield our thoughts to Christ and labor to bring our lives into conformity with his word we must daily claim boldness to take advantage of *every* relationship and *every* encounter for Christ.

So often we find ourselves in the position of being "V-8 Christians." After we have stood in line talking with another person, sat casually chatting with someone on an airplane, entertained a new neighbor in our home or attended a business luncheon in which a new deal was consummated, we hear ourselves saying, "I should have taken the time to witness to that person!" And like the people in the vegetable-juice commercials we resolve not to miss the next opportunity.

However, evangelism is such that, given other things to do, most of us will choose anything else over speaking to another person about Jesus. If we are to have a truly witnessing way of life we must seize on every opportunity the Lord gives us for sharing Jesus with others.

We must begin our day in prayer concerning the

people we are likely to meet, asking God to prepare them and us for evangelistic encounter. We must pray while we are with others, both that God would open a door for evangelism and that he would give us the boldness and the power we will need. And we must go straight ahead as the Lord leads, testifying boldly, gladly and sensitively concerning the renewing and forgiving grace of the Lord Jesus Christ.

It is difficult to imagine what might be the result if everyone who names the name of Jesus would resolve from this moment forward to cultivate a witnessing way of life. We dare to think that God's Spirit might explode in a new revival of light and life. We dare to contemplate a world turned upside down!

Why not?

Review Questions

1. What is the difference between doing evangelism and being a witness?
2. What does Jesus promise to those who are willing to deny themselves for his sake?
3. What kinds of things are included in our outlook on life?
4. Who is the new self that Christians are increasingly to put on?
5. What to do we mean by a V-8 Christian?
6. Describe the role of prayer in learning to capitalize on witnessing opportunities.

Discussion Questions

1. Take some time now to share your outline of the gospel with another person. Try to make it conversational and personal—bringing in Scripture, as you are able, to support the points you make.

2. What are some of the chief obstacles to developing a witnessing way of life?

3. How can believers help one another to become more consistent witnesses, both in their lifestyle and in personal evangelism?

4. What do you perceive to be your greatest need at this time if you are to enter fully into God's good-news way of life?

12

Where Do We Go from Here?

Well, we've said just about everything we need to say concerning the importance of becoming active and effective witnesses for the risen Lord Jesus Christ. If God's good news is going to be known throughout our neighborhoods and communities it will depend on people like you and me to get the job done. And this will require us to develop a witnessing way of life such as we described in the last chapter, with a clear understanding of the message and the most effective ways in which we might bring it.

Yet, as we mentioned earlier, the development of a witnessing way of life is not something that happens either automatically or overnight. We must persist if we are to become all that we have been recreated in Christ Jesus to be. In this chapter we want to take a look at personal Christian development so that our outlook on life and our manner of living can help us witness effectively to every person that God brings into our lives.

Grow in Grace

The place to begin charting a course of personal Christian development is with "growing in grace." What do we mean by this idea and how can we attain it?

That growing in grace is of the utmost importance for every believer goes without saying. For the apostle Peter, writing to the persecuted churches of Asia Minor, this was his most important counsel, the pastoral advice left for last in order that it might be clearly remembered and taken to heart:

> But grow in grace, and in the knowledge of our Lord and Saviour Jesus Christ. To him be glory both now and for ever. Amen (2 Pet. 3:18).

Peter knew that in the midst of their greatest trials these troubled believers could do no better than to concentrate their energies on growing in knowledge and experience of the living Lord Jesus Christ. If this was true for their witness to Jesus it must be equally true for ours. To be truly effective in telling others about Jesus we need to be increasing in our own understanding and experience of him.

Such growth in grace comes through faithful and consistent use of the means of growth which God has put at our disposal—the Bible, prayer, worship, fellowship and witnessing. To the extent that we are faithful in applying ourselves to these tools we can expect true Christian growth to occur.

How is it with each of us in this matter of Christian growth? What are our Bible-study patterns like? How fervent and consistent are our prayers? How genuine is our worship and how rich and selfless are our fellowship and care for the rest of the body of Christ? And how eagerly do we look forward to the next opportunity to tell another about the Lord? Only as we avail ourselves of these instruments of growth can we expect that God will nurture the outlook, the lifestyle and the boldness which the witnessing way of life requires. Let us resolve to establish personal growth in grace through faithful use of the means of growth which God has put at our disposal.

Grow in Favor

A second area of personal growth is suggested in Luke 2:52. Here we are told that the Lord Jesus grew in favor with God and man.

Now as we carefully use the means of growth in grace which the Lord has given us we can be assured that our inner self will be increasingly renewed according to the pattern established in Jesus. Furthermore our renewed inner self will, if we are persistent, begin more and more to bring our outer self into conformity with the changed life which is developing from within. Such reformed lifestyle cannot help but bring us increasingly into favor with God. As he looks upon us, searching out our motives, he will be more and more pleased to see the very image of his Son being expressed through our lives. As we capitalize on every opportunity to have Jesus live his life in and through us we will be changed by the power of God's Spirit with ever-increasing glory into the likeness of Jesus Christ (2 Cor. 3:18). This will draw us ever closer to our heavenly Father.

There remains the matter of growing in favor with men. We must make certain that our growing Christian experience includes adequate resources for making a positive impact on at least some of the people around us. It is impossible to think that we could live so that everyone we meet will be enthralled with us and eager to listen to the message of grace that we bring. Nevertheless we have a responsibility to do everything within our power to make our lifestyles and our relating to others as attractive as possible without compromising the distinctives of our faith (1 Cor. 9:19-23; 2 Cor. 2:15, 16).

How then can we do this?

I remember once hearing Howard Hendricks say, "Make yourself an interesting person." I find this extremely good advice. People gravitate toward interesting people. They want to talk with them, find out their impressions and opinions and be associated with them. One of the greatest shortcomings of many Christians seems to be that they simply are not very interesting. Sweet—yes; considerate—certainly; but not very interesting. What makes a person interesting?

An interesting person, it seems to me, is one who is well informed. He or she has a sense of what is going on in the world and is able to talk intelligently about a wide range of subjects. It's not very interesting continually to be saying in the midst a conversation, "I don't know, what do you think?" Christians have a responsibility to keep broadly informed concerning the issues and events of today's world, as well as various fields of knowledge. This is, after all, God's world and we are his people in it. It ill behooves us therefore to act with indifference or ignorance concerning our Father's world.

Interesting people tend also to be somewhat opinionated. Because they come at life from a well-thought-out world view they are able to make up their own minds and give persuasive reasons for their opinions. In being opinionated they need not be obnoxious; rather the firmness of their opinions can enable them to be tolerant and cordial toward the opinions of others, for they will not be easily threatened or intimidated.

Interesting people also know how to appreciate others and to make them feel important. How many times have you come away from meeting a new person feeling that this is someone you really like, someone you'd like to get to know better, only to discover upon further reflection that you spent your initial time together talking mainly about yourself? Interesting people are interested in others —in who they are, what they think, and what they believe—and they are willing to encourage others to talk freely about themselves and their lives. How interesting are you when it comes to making others feel important or significant?

There are many other things we could say about becoming an interesting person. Interesting people have a good sense of humor; they enjoy the fellowship of others; they are willing to try new foods, new places, new friendships; and they try to take a generally creative approach to living. Each of us could stand to become more interesting. To the extent that we apply ourselves to this task we can expect that our favor in the sight of others will begin to increase.

Grow in Perseverance

One of the most reliable measures of a person's effectiveness at any task is the degree of perseverance he or she brings to it. The same can be said of developing a witnessing way of life. Is this a matter we are willing to persevere at regardless of how many times we fail, how difficult it may be or how fearful we may be from time to time? Unless we are convinced that it is we will approach this matter in just the same way we do so many others: we'll get excited about it for a time, give it our best shot for a brief period, encounter difficulties and trials, and begin looking for some new area of ministry.

It is a regrettable fact that very often we Christians do not have enough stick-to-itiveness to convince anyone of the sincerity of our faith or the urgency of the matters with which our faith is concerned. Because of this and because of the enormous importance of the task of making God's good news known, we must persevere at developing a witnessing way of life, regardless of the cost.

But how can we begin to do that?

Again, as in so many other matters, the place to begin is in prayer. We must daily implore our heavenly Father to develop in us a witnessing way of life. We must pray for boldness; we must ask God to make us alert to the opportunities to witness that daily confront us; and we must pray that we may become the kind of interesting persons to whom others will want to listen. Whatever witnessing we are able to accomplish will be vacuous and devoid of true passion for the lost unless that witnessing has its beginnings in prayer.

A second critical ingredient for perseverance is alertness to the promptings of God's Spirit. I do not mean to suggest that the Holy Spirit either speaks openly to us or sends revelatory messages advising us of opportunities before us. At the same time, however, we are all acquainted with what I mean by this matter of the prompting of God's Spirit. You are having lunch with a new friend, talking casually about this or that, when suddenly something he says trips a switch in your mind and the thought enters, "He needs to hear the gospel." What do you do at that point? The persevering believer takes such promptings seriously and begins to work the conversation in a direction of a brief, clear presentation of the gospel. The weak believer merely shrugs off such promptings, reckoning that his friend probably would not be interested anyway. This should not happen!

Finally, and following directly from this, perseverance flows out of courageous obedience. When called upon to bear witness in a courtroom the subpoenaed person has no choice but to go forward, take his appointed place and tell what he knows concerning the question at hand. So often I find Christian witnesses ducking behind the benches, heading for the doors or even denying that they know anything at all in the face of the call to present their testimony. Such spineless conduct must not characterize those who are seeking to develop a witnessing way of life. Immediate, unquestioning obedience to what the situation requires is our only option as believers.

Developing a witnessing way of life requires more than merely learning a simple presentation of the gospel and sharing it with others on a regular basis. It requires growth in grace, growth in favor with others and growth in perseverance. Are we up to the challenge of a witnessing way of life?

Review Questions

1. What tools has God given us to help us grow in grace?
2. How do we know that Peter considered that growing in grace was a matter of primary importance?
3. What does it mean to be increasing in favor with men?
4. What are some of the characteristics of an interesting person?
5. Explain the role of prayer in persevering to develop a witnessing way of life.
6. How is obedience related to perseverance?

Discussion Questions

1. Take some time to practice your conversational presentation of the gospel with someone else at this time. Concentrate on sharing—not reciting—the good news of Jesus Christ.

2. Discuss your personal Bible study and devotional patterns. How might they be improved? What would you like to see different? What problems are you encountering? How is prayer related to your Bible study? What other areas of your own growth in grace need some attention?

3. What are some things you might be interested in doing to start becoming a more interesting person? Who are the people most likely to be affected by your growing in this area of your life?

4. Take some time to share with another person or in a small group an occasion when you felt that God was prompting you to witness to another person. What was the setting? How did you become aware of God's prompting? How did you respond? How could you improve on that experience for the next such situation?

13

What Is the Role of the Church in Making God's Good News Known?

Our concern in this study has been to set forth the mandate for making God's good news known by his people, as well as to prepare and urge each of us to undertake that responsibility as a way of life. We have sought to show the importance of the gospel for bringing new meaning and hope to the men and women of our forlorn generation. We have pointed out the divine directive that makes the members of the believing community responsible for evangelizing their neighbors. And we have encouraged the idea that truly effective evangelism is best accomplished in the normal contexts and through the natural relationships of our everyday lives.

In this final chapter we need to consider the role of the local church in this overall effort. We must not think that making God's good news known is the responsibility only of isolated individuals; rather we must see the evangelistic task as a part of a total community process in which the church as a body has a vital role to play. Only when the local church has become committed to accepting its role in fulfilling God's Great Commission will individual lifestyle evangelists be enabled to carry out their particular work.

It is then to a consideration of the role of the local church in making God's good news known that we now turn our attention.

The Church as Training Ground

The first role which the church must fulfill is as a training ground for witnesses for Jesus Christ. In this regard some clear patterns of development are delineated in the New Testament.

According to the apostle Paul in Ephesians 4:11-15 three primary features of the church's equipping role may be discerned. First, there is the central role of the pastor as the leader in equipping others. Paul says that God has given some to be pastors and teachers to prepare his people for works of service. The word "perfecting" (vs. 12) can be just as well translated "equip." The meaning seems quite clear: the Lord has placed pastors in the church for the purpose of equipping others to carry on the work of the Kingdom.

We normally tend to think that the pastor was given to the church in order to do the work of the Kingdom by himself, but this is clearly not what Paul indicates here. Pastors are to equip men and women for the work of the Kingdom.

The first point of the church's role as training ground, therefore, has to do with the central significance of pastors as equippers of others. No church can expect to succeed in this important work without a pastor who is willing and able to function in this kind of position.

Second, there is the role of the people in performing the work of service. So often, as I have indicated, we support the idea that people are to be served by professional clergy. This pattern is reflected in so many churches, yet it is contrary to what Paul envisions here. People are to be equipped by pastors so that they might assume the responsibility of the work of the Kingdom themselves.

No church can expect to fulfill its earthly reason for being when its people are unwilling or unable to accept the responsibility for the work of the Kingdom. For their part, therefore, the people of God in the local church must make themselves available for the training which faithful and able ministers seek to bring to them (cf. 2 Tim. 2:2).

Finally, we must see from this passage that one of the climactic goals of the equipping process is that the people learn to speak the truth in love (vs. 15). Whatever else this means it certainly carries the connotation that high on the list is the ability to declare the gospel in a loving manner to lost friends and neighbors. "Speaking the truth in love" appears in this passage as the acme of the equipping process—that toward which everything else seems to tend.

No church can be said to be fulfilling its role if it is not actively seeking to equip the saints for the work of lifestyle evangelism under the active leadership of responsible pastors. This is the first and most basic role of the church under the evangelistic mandate of the gospel.

The Church as Base of Operations

The second role of the local church is as a base of operations for the spread of the gospel. Throughout the New
Testament it is evident that the community of believers
took a central role in praying together and encouraging
one another in sharing God's good news with the people
in their area. We see the Jerusalem Christians, in the face
of threats from the government, praying together and going to bear witness in the boldness of the Holy Spirit
(Acts 4:23-33). The Christians in Antioch evidently became so vocal for the Lord Jesus that they came to be
called by his name (Acts 11:26). Paul commended the believers in Thessalonica for the way their testimony to the
Lord Jesus had reached everywhere (1 Thess. 1:8). And
the church at Antioch was careful to make time for those
involved in outreach to report the results to the rest of the
congregation (Acts 14:26, 27).

A significant aspect of the body life of those early
churches was concerned with preparation for and involvement in evangelism. The local congregation seems
to have served as the staging ground for evangelistic
operations in cities throughout the Mediterranean world.
Our own churches will be something less than effective if
they fail to serve in this capacity. We must consider how
the local church in our day can fulfill this aspect of its
evangelistic role in the community. What will this require
of our church's governing boards? How will such an obli-
gation affect our church budget? What kinds of expectations does this imply for new members just coming into
the church? And what kinds of new entry into the com-

munity will our churches need if they are going to serve as bases of operations for lifestyle evangelism? All these questions and more besides will need to be addressed by local churches if they are to fulfill the role for which they have been created.

The Church as Nurturing Bosom

The final role that seems to be important is that of a nurturing bosom for new believers and all the members of the congregation. In the early church new Christians could get a proper grounding in the Bible, prayer, worship and the fellowship of believers. The local church served to ground new believers in the means of growth that we discussed in our last chapter (cf. Acts 2:41-47). At the same time, older believers were helped to grow in their faith, part of which involved being equipped for service.

Our churches must serve in the same role. They must be places to which new believers can be brought to begin their life in Christ on a proper footing. Churches must provide contexts in which new believers can be adequately nourished. Special classes for new Christians will need to be sponsored. Opportunities for new members to get to know one another and the other members of the congregation will need to be provided. Effective pastoral oversight will need to be given to discover and meet the needs of new believers and their families.

A total, balanced ministry of teaching, caring, worshiping, and serving one another will need to be put in place in our local churches. Only healthy, balanced churches can sustain active outreach in their communities. Thus, we must commit ourselves to establishing such an arrangement within our own churches.

The church cannot become the base of operations for community outreach unless it takes seriously its role of equipping the saints. This will not happen unless a context for Christian nurture has been provided. The three roles of the local church are intimately related to one another. The whole dynamic of church life is incomplete without all three. They lead logically into one another and together make for a church where the gospel is faithfully declared and God's people are carefully equipped for making God's good news known throughout the communities of our land. As responsible members of the church of Jesus Christ we must not rest until our own local church has begun to address each of these roles. Only thus can we be assured of a context which will encourage and support the critical work of lifestyle evangelism on the part of the people of God.

Review Questions

1. Who is responsible to take the leading role in equipping others for the work of the Kingdom in a local church?

2. What is the role of the people with respect to the work of ministry in a local church?

3. What do we mean by the local church serving as a base of operations for evangelistic outreach?

4. What is required of local churches for beginning to nurture new believers?

5. Explain how the three primary roles of the local church are related to one another.

Discussion Questions

1. Take some time now to practice your conversational presentation of the gospel. Again concentrate on sharing God's good news, not on reciting an outline.

2. What do you suppose are some reasons that so few churches seem to be fulfilling their roles in the evangelistic work of the Kingdom? Where are the breakdowns? What can be done about this situation?

3. Why do you suppose Paul puts such primary emphasis on the equipping role of the pastor in Eph. 4:11-15?

4. What kind of equipping for speaking the truth in love exists within your own church? If you could design an

ideal equipping ministry what might it include? See what the following verses suggest in this regard:

1) –Mark 3:14   4) –Matt. 5:1, 2

2) –Luke 9:1–6   5) –Luke 10:1, 2

3) –2 Tim. 2:2

1) Jesus appointed 12 to be with him and he would send them out to preach

2) Jesus gave them power & authority to do miracles & he sent them out to preach & heal

3) Paul tells Timothy to teach reliable men what PAUL taught him so they can teach others

4) Jesus went to be alone with his disciples & taught them, be ATTitudes

5) Jesus appointed 72 & sent them out in PAIRS ahead of him where he WAS going to go, The harvest is plenty but workers are few ASK the Lord for workers to be sent out